Art Therapy
Extraordinary
Gardens

100 DESIGNS
COLOURING IN AND RELAXATION

illustrated by **Sophie Leblanc**

jacqui
small

First published in the UK, USA and Australia in 2015
Jacqui Small LLP
74–77 White Lion Street
London N1 9PF

Text © 2014 Jacqui Small LLP

First published by Hachette Livre (Hachette Pratique), 2014
© Hachette Livre (Hachette Pratique), 2013

Illustrations: Sophie Leblanc
Translation: Hilary Mandleberg

ISBN: 978 1 910254 06 6

10 9 8 7 6 5 4 3 2 1

Printed in China

Preface

Discover the joy of liberating your mind and delight in the slow observation of nature. Ever since the Garden of Eden, gardens have been symbols of peace and pleasure. And since antiquity, they have been a sign of civilization, too. In the third century before Christ, Gilgamesh, the semi-mythic king of Uruk in the Epic of Gilgamesh, laid out the most fabulous gardens in his magnificent city. But it was in Babylon that the most famous ancient gardens of all – the Hanging Gardens of Babylon – were constructed, by order of king Nebuchadnezzar II. Said to have consisted of wooded terraces, they were one of the Seven Wonders of the World.

The pages of this book will take your imagination on a journey through time and the seasons. It won't be long before you imagine yourself as a great gardener to the king, designing the most beautiful French-style parterres, formal gardens just as André Le Nôtre laid out Louis XIV's famous gardens at Versailles. Or perhaps you'll see yourself as a landscaper extraordinaire, like eighteenth-century English landscape architect, Capability Brown; or as an explorer-botanist, creating some exotic herb garden; or simply as a far-flung sage meditating beneath his tree.

These 100 original designs have been devised for you to colour in. They offer your imagination and creativity a world of calming, pleasure-filled landscapes. Choose from labyrinths of vegetation, extraordinary topiary effects, elegant, romantic gardens, friezes of tulips that evoke the Taj Mahal, roses worthy of watercolours by Pierre-Joseph Redouté, and Liberty-style plantings bestrewn with flowers. But that isn't all: birds and insects also play their part, helping to create quiet, intimate scenes that combine plumage, foliage and blossom.

Patrice Fustier of the Domaine de Courson

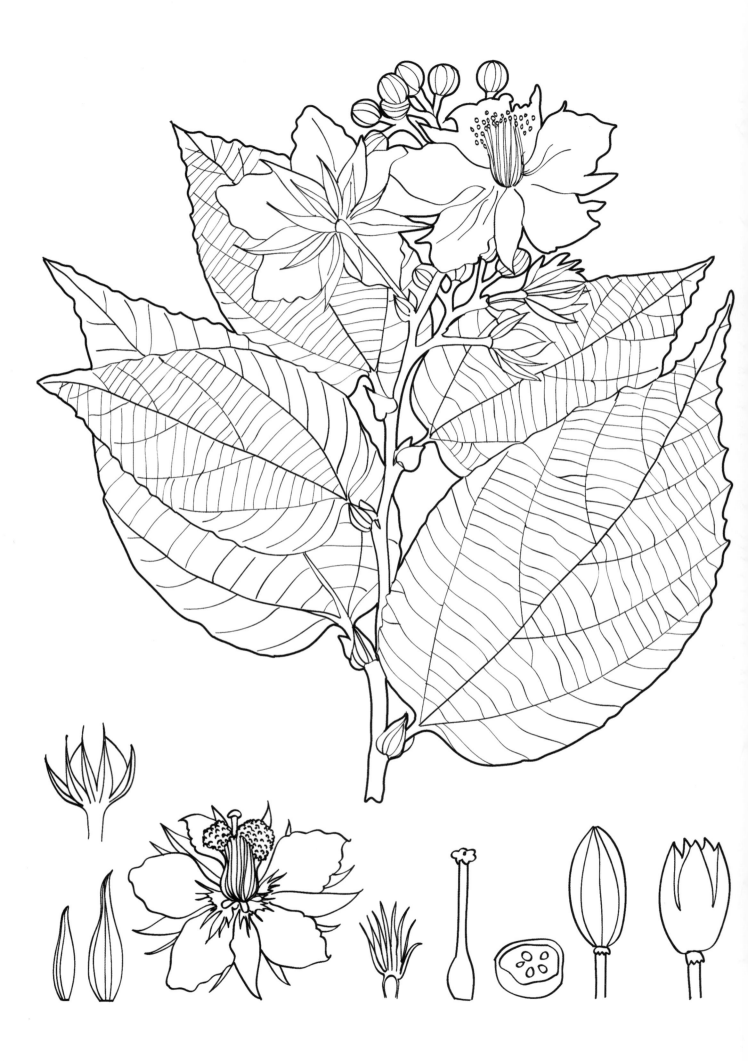

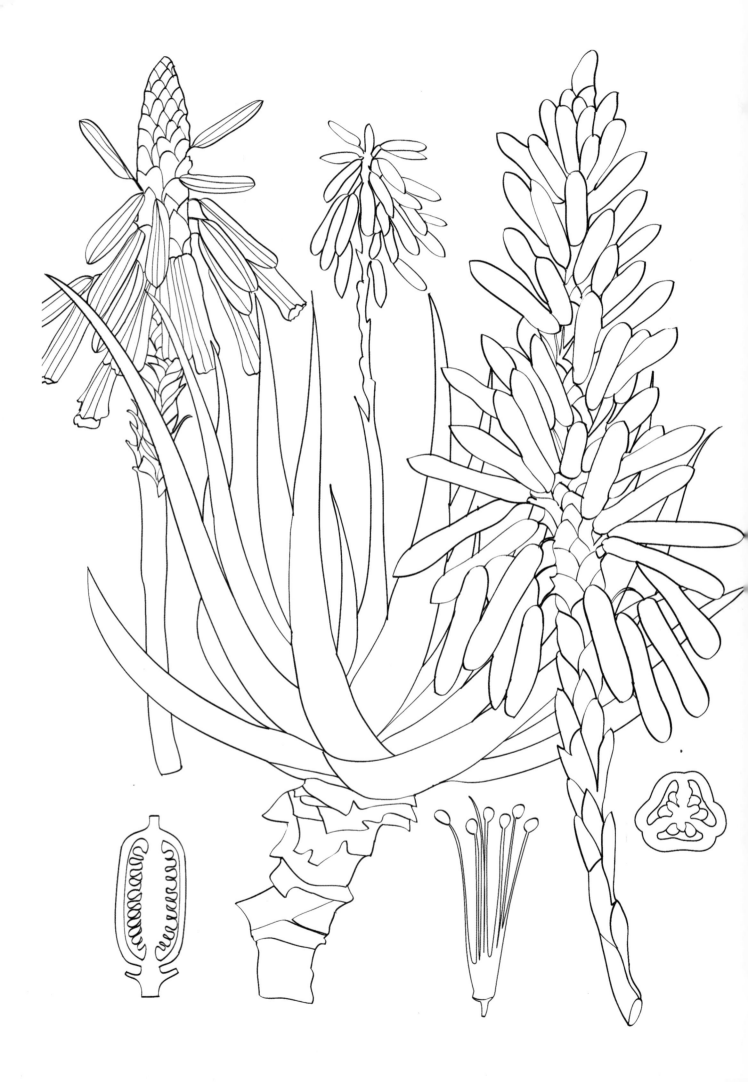

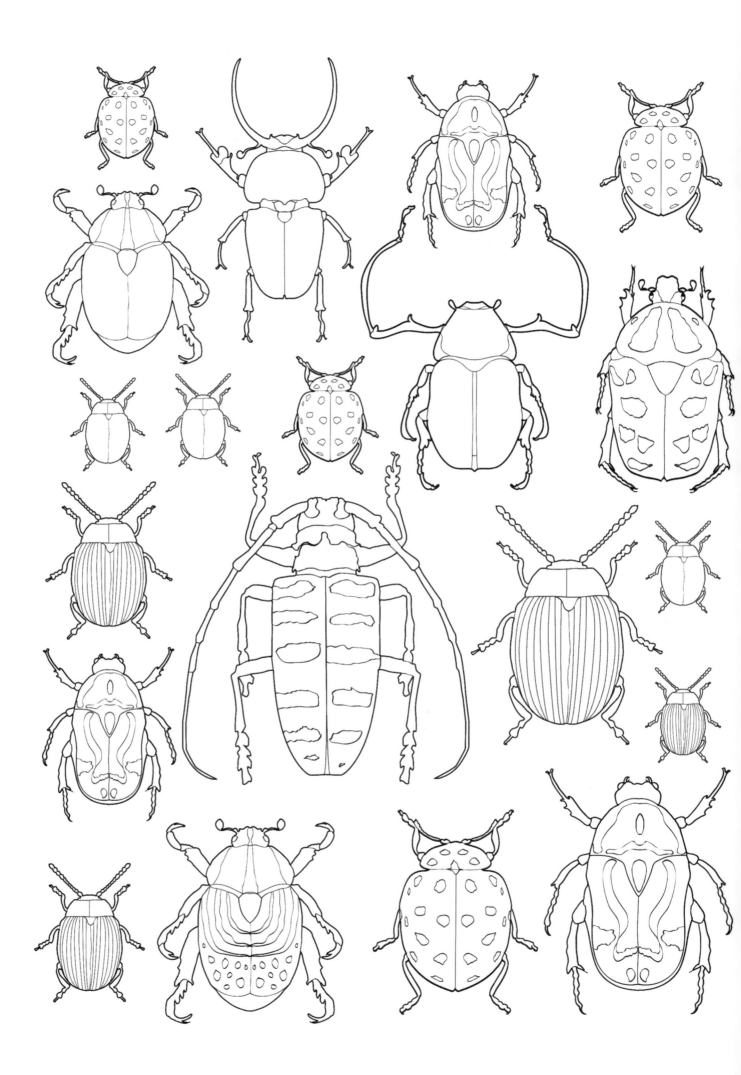

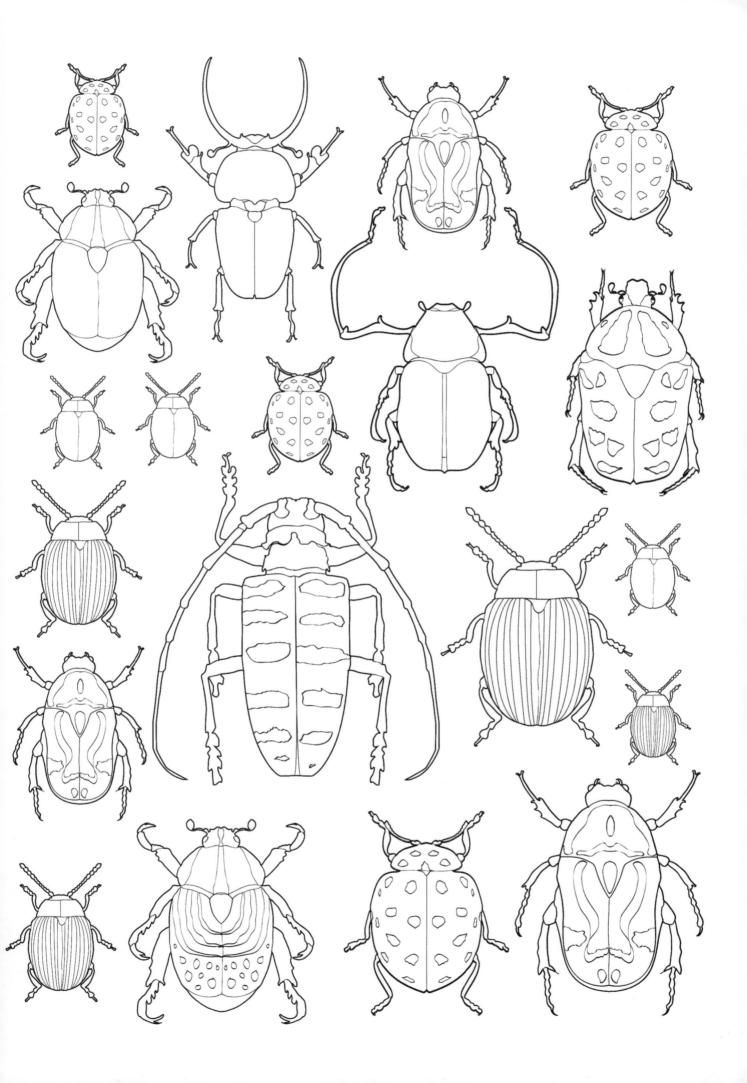

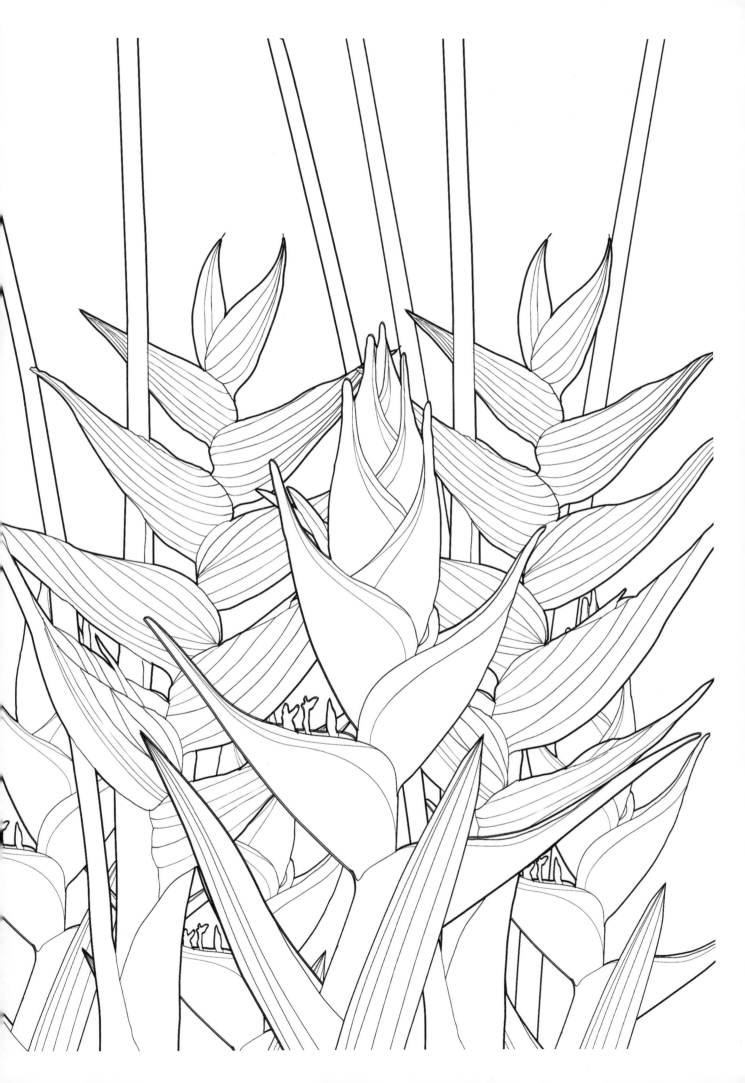

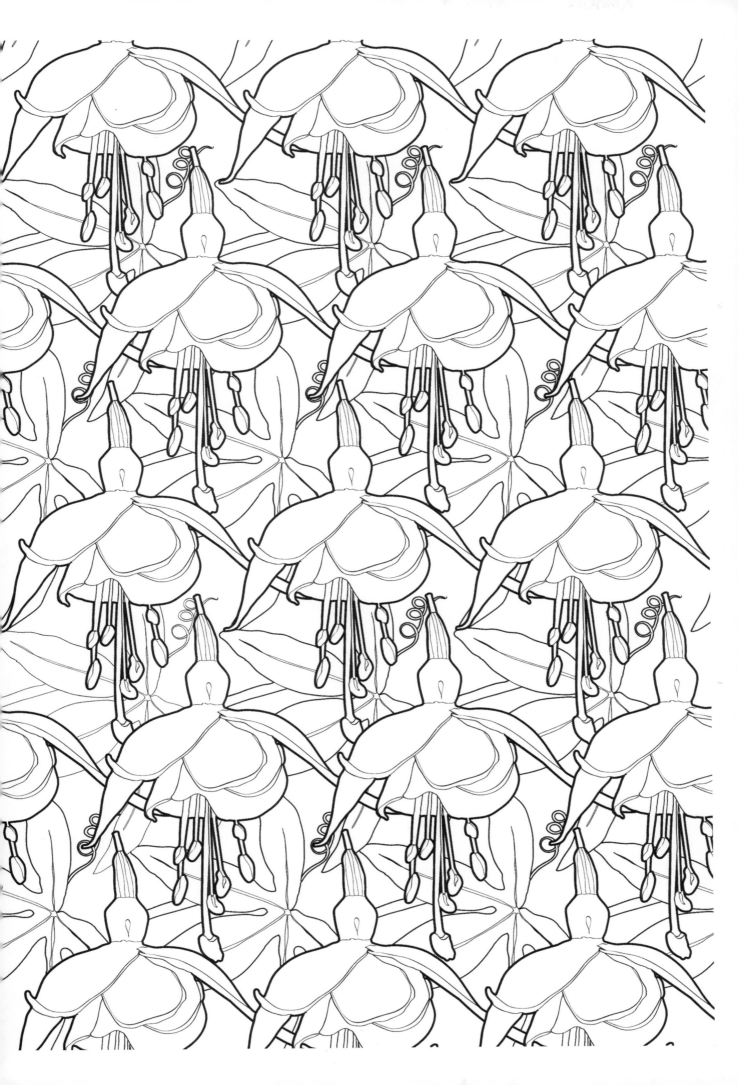

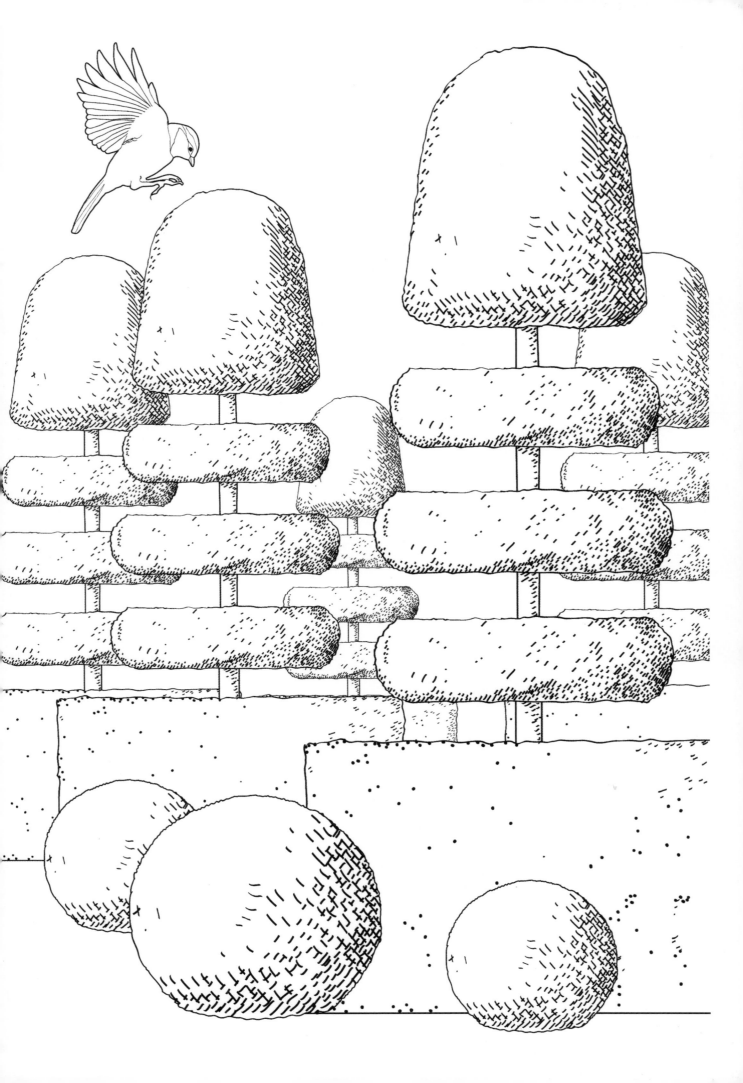

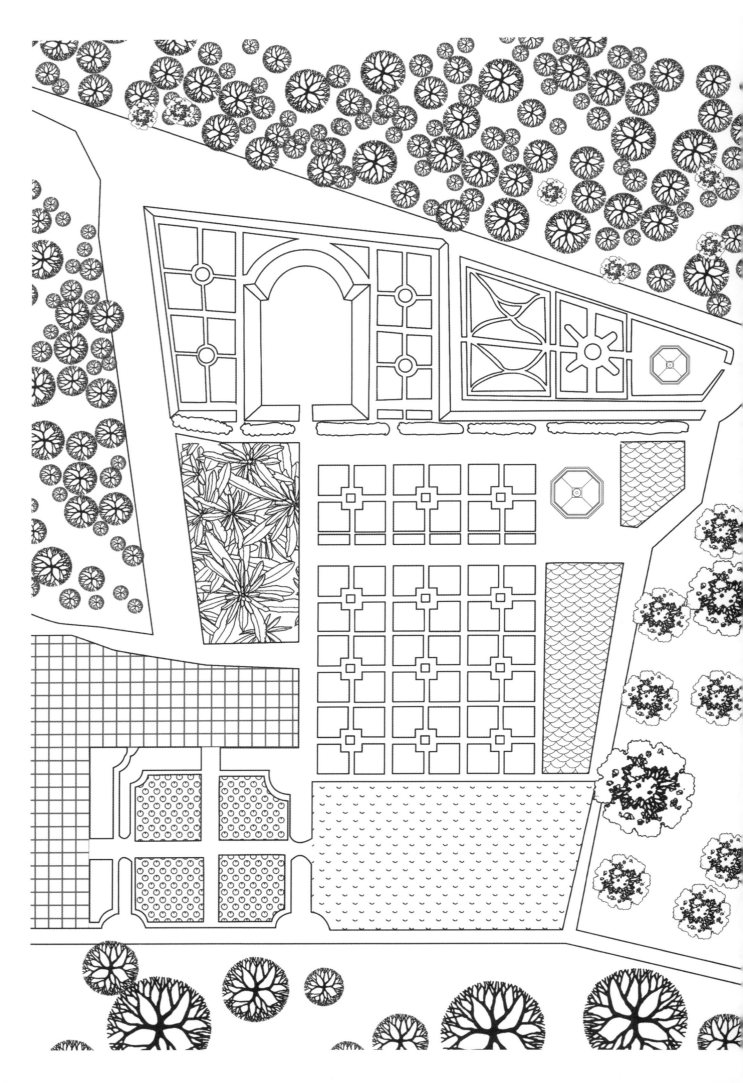

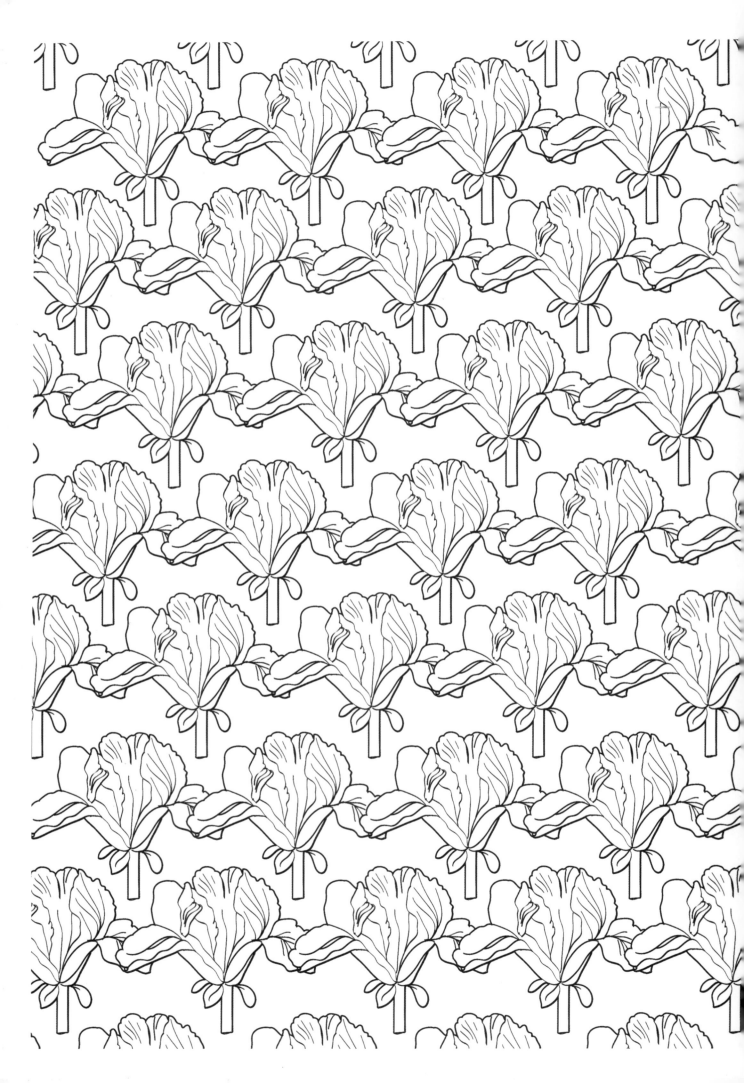